50 POWERFUL

COACHING QUESTIONS

TO HELP BUILD

CLIENT ENGAGEMENT

A guide for entrepreneurs who want to create successful and profitable relationships in business

DR. LIZ MUSIL

COPYRIGHT & PERMISSIONS

DR. LIZ MUSIL

INTRODUCTION

FEW BUSINESSES KNOW ABOUT THE WONDERS OF CLIENT
ENGAGEMENT VIA THOROUGH AND PERSONABLE COMMUNICATION,
AND EVEN FEWER STILL TRULY AND EFFECTIVELY TAKE ADVANTAGE OF
THIS OPPORTUNITY. TODAY, WE WILL DISCUSS JUST THAT; CLIENT
ENGAGEMENT THROUGH COMMUNICATION, FURTHER ELUCIDATING ON
THE NECESSITY OF HEALTHY INTERACTIONS, TEAM BUILDING,
EMOTIONAL INTELLIGENCE, AND HOW TECHNOLOGY FITS INTO ALL THIS.

Fifty powerful coaching questions to help build client engagement

By: Dr Liz Musil

For what it's worth, the Internet has created opportunity. Such is a generally an undisputed fact. It has disseminated knowledge to previously unimaginable locations, rekindled distant relationships, and expanded the horizons for businesses worldwide. However, there is one aspect of business which the Internet has not helped with; communication. With customers from all over the world able to do business at any time and at any place, it is no wonder that businessperson-to-customer relationship has lost its personality. One of the most neglected aspects of online and offline businesses are client engagement through communication.

BUILDING CLIENT ENGAGEMENT THROUGH COMMUNICATION

Few businesses know about the wonders of client engagement via thorough and personable communication, and even fewer still truly and effectively take advantage of this opportunity. Today, we will discuss just that; client engagement through communication, further elucidating on the necessity of healthy interactions, team building, emotional intelligence, and how technology fits into all this.

A news article that includes Interaction with one's customers is extremely important. Communicating effectively, politely, and thoroughly is a key to having satisfied customers that are eager to conduct repeat business. Most businesses generally do a decent job of reporting information to their customers in a stoic and impersonal way, and while that is better than no communication at all, having quality client engagement will put the businesses ahead of the game. Building relationships and familiarity with your clients separates you from the competition. How is this client engagement that was alluded to in the previous sentence achieved?

Well, there are several ways you can substantially increase client engagement. Perhaps most obviously, interaction and dialogue between customers can do a great deal of good for your businesses. By discussing the particulars of a product or service with clients and doing so meticulously you necessarily encourage client engagement and furthermore prompt the customer to remember the interaction. Typically, when customers purchase a product or service, they do not tend to dedicate much thought to the entity from which they purchased the product or service. By affably engaging with your customers and making the interactions thorough, simple, and pleasant, you will likely make your customers remember the ease through which they attained the product or service and thereby look upon your business with favor. Overall, interacting with one's clients is a near-perfect way to bring favorable attention to your business that lasts in your customer's minds.

Aside from interactions, which are likely the most obviously necessary commodity on the list, let us look to team building, which is perhaps more intuitive.

Building strong relationships with your clients via teamwork and corroboration will also go a long way in aiding your business endeavors. Unfortunately, many businesses lazily neglect helping their customers with the products or services they offer. This leaves the customer confused and often times disappointed due to a lack of knowledge about the product or service. By working with your clients and helping them understand products and services - rather than blindly shoving those products and service down their throat - you make customers feel engaged and empowered, willing to do business with you again. A simple explication of the purpose and nature of your product will usually not suffice. Rather, person-to-person communication is the absolute most effective way to convey the particulars of your product or service; how it's used, and what it will achieve. It is very clear that by building strong business relations with your clients and working alongside them can potentially have great ramifications for your business. By doing this effectively, one can create a bountiful environment for your business, one that will never cease to draw eyes and create business. A blog article can include examples of the interaction with clients and testimonials. Communicating effectively, politely, and thoroughly is a key to having satisfied customers that are anxious to conduct repeat business. Most businesses generally do a decent job of providing basic information on a website, and while that is better than no communication at all, having quality client engagement will put the businesses that use it far ahead of the game. How is this client engagement that was alluded to in the previous sentence achieved?

However, these two aspects, while very good, do not represent a full picture of client engagement. By exemplifying wholesome virtues such as patience and trust and by connecting with your clients emotionally via strong emotional intelligence you can likewise create a pleasant environment which your clients will be anxious to utilize. What does this mean? Well, by emotional intelligence, we essentially are referring to people skills.

When dealing with clients, businesses often make the unintentional and, for the most part, innocent mistake of believing emotional connections is something to be eschewed in the business world. On the contrary, emotional connection is one of the most critical facets. This skill, often called; "emotional intelligence" is generally split into five categories; self-awareness, self-regulation, motivation, empathy, and people skills. These five skills are extremely important for the health of your business. Emotionalintelligenceatwork.com powerfully states that; "Emotional intelligence is applicable to every human interaction in business; from staff motivation to customer service, from brainstorming to company presentations." So even if you are not convinced that emotional intelligence is important in regards to customer-businessman relations, you should still value it in the workplace for it value among employee-employee interactions.

Finally, we have the most important question of the day; how does technology fit into all this? With a world leaning more and more heavily on the powers of the Internet and technology, it may appear that personal interaction is rendered unnecessary. Nothing could be further from the truth. At the end of the day, confidence and simplicity are still confidence and simplicity with or without technology. Imparting feelings of confidence and empowerment to your customers is still equally important. By using real people rather than answering machines, and by having an affable employee base that is technologically adept, you can still retain the personal engagement that clients enjoy while still remaining wholly adept in regards to technology. In the end, endeavoring to engage your customers is a never failing strategy that will have all sorts of beneficial results on your company. By applying the steps outlined here, your business can become renowned for its quality service and genial staff without losing the technological aptitude your business also needs. At the end of the day, we strongly recommend you take the time to integrate further client engagement in your business so that you can see the beneficial results as many companies around the world have.

BUILDING BUSINESS RELATIONSHIPS THROUGH INTERACTIVE QUESTIONS

A business is an entity that can only be successful with help of people. Those people can be your clients and they can be your employees too. Here we are going to focus upon the relationship you built with your clients. Sometime your client leaves you, and you are unaware of why. One of the most important role is to maintain and enhance relationships with them. I am going to give you some quick suggestions that are going to help you foster important, lasting business relationships.

Creating a collaborative relationship with clients

The first and the foremost thing is that what do we need to build collaborative relationships with our clients. Relationship with client is the most important element as the client is the one due to which you are going to earn money. If you will not have some good and healthy relationship with your clients then you might not be able to run a successful business in the market.

Be clear and understanding

The word collaboration means when you consider others person's needs. If you are willing to listen other people views and suggestions then you will be in a better position to judge the conclusion. This way you might be able to give the client much more plausible insights, ideas and solutions. You need to ensure that the client is clear about what he wants otherwise it might end up as a disaster.

Ensure communication is two way

You need to ensure that the client is comfortable communicating with you. Basically collaboration is two way while communication is one way. To collaborate with clients you need to communicate well with them.

Focus on the customer

The company needs to focus upon the customers so that they provide them the best service. The company should be customer-oriented, rather than company-cantered. This act is going to give you the liberty of developing a collaborative relationship with customers. This way your customers are going to get a chance to co create with your organization. This is going to help drive up th company's position in the market.

How to use questions and their responses to build trust

Questions are a good way to clarify what the client is trying to say. Sometimes the clients are not clear about what they want so at that moment it is the duty of the employee to provide the client with a perfect suggestion. But before providing any suggestion the employees needs to ask some basic questions so that the needs of the client are clear. This way the employee will be able to give a better solution.

Using online tools to strengthen your professional image

Online tools have provided a cushion to the businesses to improve. There are a lot of tools that aid in building customer business relationship. Online tools such as email generator could help businesses to grow as this way the clients will remain in touch with the latest updates. In addition to this technology brings in much more accuracy into the records. The data is much more secure and the transaction time reduces. These are all the factors that are ultimately going to help the client in a positive manner. When he will witness efficient services he is definitely going to get impressed and recommend your company to others. The more the clients you have the more you are going to build a strong reputation.

Growing your reputation among clients & attracting new ones

Growing your brand reputation among clients is not difficult because you understand, validate, and support their success.

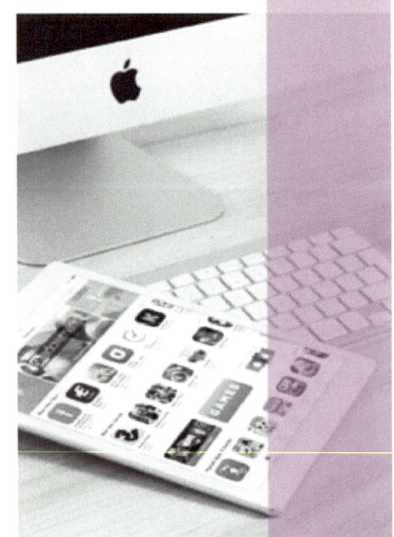

Engage prospective clients and new clients by learning their expectations, wants, and needs

Clients get satisfied when you fulfil what they want and according to the way they want these services. This way you will be able to make new clients. Prospective clients are the customers that have the potential to be your client but they need a little bit of persuasion and motivation. You can engage prospective employees by explaining them the benefits of and the positives of the product that you are marketing. Before explaining the clients what you are offering to them you need to give a chance to the clients to talk about their expectations. This way you will be able to mold the benefits of your products in such a way that it would make the client think that this is the perfect product for him. This way the client will be able to fulfil his expectations and you will be able to sell your product.

Using questions to measure client satisfaction

After you sell a product you need to make sure that the client is satisfied with the product you delivered. This way the client will feel that the company feels for him and the client will feel himself more secure. The way through which you will make the client feel satisfied is by asking him certain questions about the service or the product you delivered. This way you will get to know about the client's satisfaction level and you will be able to get to know the drawbacks and the flaws in your own service that needs to be overcome.

THE
GROW
MODEL OF
COACHING

GOAL

REALITY

OPTIONS

WAY FORWARD

GROW

The GROW Model of coaching is a purposeful framework used by executive coaches. GROW helps clients learn about themselves, improve performance, solve problems, learn new skills, and reach goals. Using the GROW Model strengthens client / coach relationships. GROW is an acronym that stands for:

GOAL
REALITY (CURRENT)
OPTIONS
WAY FORWARD

Using the GROW method successfully requires the coach to skillfully ask open ended questions in all four sections of the GROW framework. Questions are rarely asked sequentially, most coaching sessions skip around to help the client achieve insight to a variety of situations. A key is that the coach is guiding the client through self-discovery, to help him or her realize actionable answers. The coach doesn't tell the client what to do, but helps influence discovery in a productive direction.

EXECUTIVE COACHING
USING THE GROW MODEL

PART ONE:
G = GOAL
HELPING SOMEONE
GET FOCUS

What overarching GOAL do you want to accomplish?

1

What result are you looking for with the assistance of coaching?

2

Why do you want to realize this goal?

3

What will be the benefits of reaching this goal? What are the possible drawbacks?

4

How will you feel if you reach this goal? How will you feel if you do not?

5

Do you believe that you have the power to make your goal a reality?

6

Are there external influences that will hinder your actions or power in realizing this goal?

7

How do you define success?

8

What do you really want?

9

Do you consider yourself a work in progress?

10

PART TWO:
R = REALITY
UNDERSTANDING
THE CURRENT
SITUATION

What actions have you taken to move towards this goal?

1

What is required of you to meet your goal? What is required of others?

2

What has contributed to your success thusfar? What has hindered you?

3

Why haven't you met your goal already? What is standing in your way?

4

What is your relationship to your goal? Can you see any blocks?

5

Do you know other people that have reached your goal?

6

What can you learn from others who have reached your goal?

7

Do you have any fears surrounding meeting your goal? How will your life change?

8

Is anything stopping your efforts from working towards your goal?

9

Is your goal realistic and attainable?

10

What can others do to support you in working towards your goal?

11

What have you already tried?

12

What have you learned from your efforts so far?

13

Have you broken your goal into action steps? Do you have a timeline?

14

Does the environment support your goal?

15

PART THREE: O = OPTIONS EXPLORING OPTIONS AND GENERATING SOLUTIONS

What are some next steps?

1

What are your options?

2

Who can help you?

3

What will happen if you do nothing?

4

What happens if you do nothing for a week?

5

How does your creativity emerge?

6

Which part is most difficult for you?

7

Which options can you act on right now?

8

What advice would you give someone else with a similar goal?

9

Are you celebrating your successes?

10

What makes you happy about working on this goal?

11

Do you have a diagram or mindmap of your goal?

12

Who can help keep you accountable to your progress?

13

What can you do today to move forward?

14

What about your mindset needs to change so you can achieve your goal?

15

PART FOUR:
W = WAY FORWARD
COMMITMENT AND
ACTION PLAN

What is next? How are we going to map out your action plan?

1

What is your level of commitment towards achieving your goal?

2

How can you increase and maintain that commitment?

3

Why will you succeed in reaching your goal?

4

Can or will you accept defeat?

5

What roadblocks do you expect?

6

What support and resources do you need to succeed?

7

What three steps will you take this week?

8

How flexible will you be in working around obstacles?

9

How motivated are you today?

10

WORKSHEETS

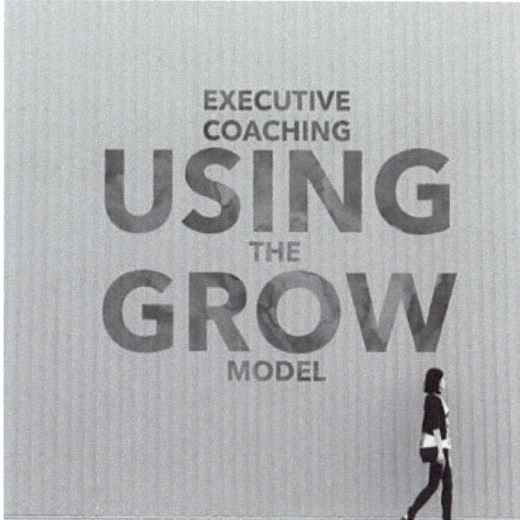

EXECUTIVE
COACHING
USING
THE
GROW
MODEL

DR. LIZ MUSIL

THE ULTIMATE LIST OF

GOALS

OVERARCHING GOAL:

ACTION STEPS AND DUE DATES:

1.

2.

3.

4.

5.

6.

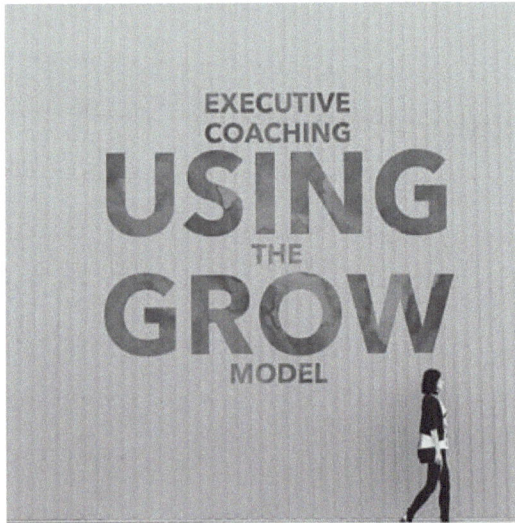

EXECUTIVE
COACHING
USING
THE
GROW
MODEL

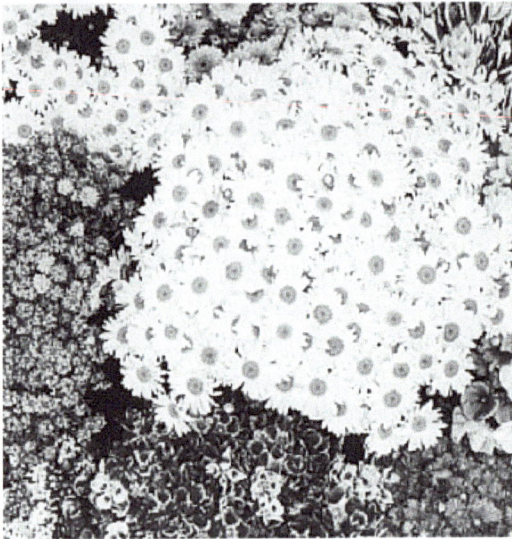

DR. LIZ MUSIL

DEVELOPING MY

MINDSET

WHAT CHANGES DO I NEED TO MAKE?

ACTION STEPS AND DUE DATES:

1.

2.

3.

4.

5.

6.

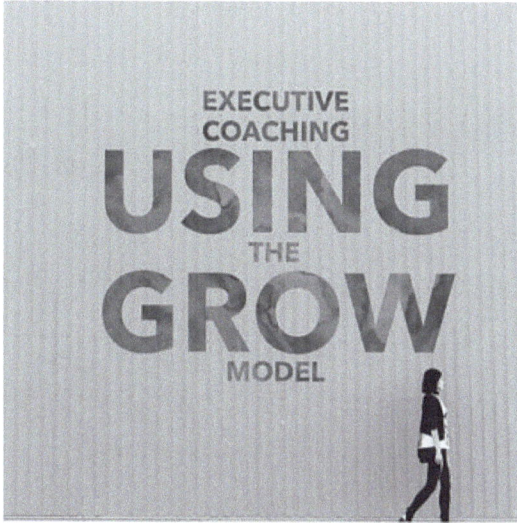

DEVELOPING MY

COMMITMENT

WHAT CAN I DO TO STRENGTHEN MY COMMITMENT?

_____

_____

_____

_____

_____

ACTION STEPS AND DUE DATES:

1.

2.

3.

4.

5.

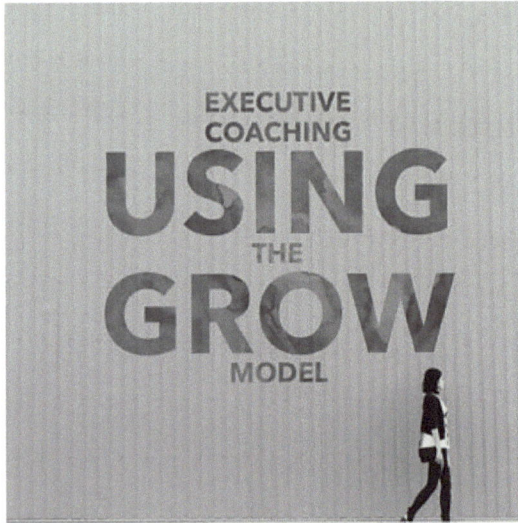

EXECUTIVE COACHING USING THE GROW MODEL

DR. LIZ MUSIL

DEVELOPING MY

CONFIDENCE

HOW CAN I INCREASE MY CONFIDENCE?

ACTION STEPS AND DUE DATES:

1.

2.

3.

4.

5.

6.

DR. LIZ MUSIL

WHAT ARE MY

NEXT STEPS?

WHAT STEPS WILL I TAKE NOW?

_____

_____

_____

_____

_____

ACTION STEPS AND DUE DATES:

1.

2.

3.

4.

5.

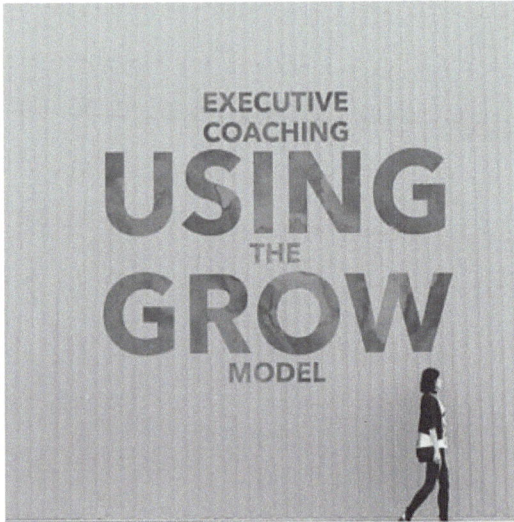

EXECUTIVE
COACHING
USING
THE
GROW
MODEL

DR. LIZ MUSIL

MEASUREMENTS OF

SUCCESS

WHAT ARE MY SUCCESSES AND HOW WILL I
BUILD ON THEM?

ACTION STEPS AND DUE DATES:

1.

2.

3.

4.

5.

ABOUT THE AUTHOR:

DR. LIZ MUSIL

Dr.Liz Musil is a virtual business coach, professor, consultant, author, public speaker and founder of Liz Musil Consultants. With over twenty years organizational, leadership, management, and technology consulting, and fifteen years' eCommerce and web development experience, Dr. Musil has an in depth understanding of leadership, management, and growth strategies for virtual organizations. She has worked in eCommerce, project management, strategy, finance, IT, and in all significant organizational capacities at the corporate level and as an external consultant.

Liz has consulted in entrepreneurial, virtual, and corporate business for over a decade in various industries such as education, banking, entertainment, music, and fashion. She also serves as an adjunct professor at several universities and has taught both in the classroom and online for over 12 years. Dr. Musil often is consulted as an instructional designer and a subject matter expert to develop online and classroom courses. Current projects include further researching Virtual Leadership attributes and creating research based assessment tools.

Dr. Liz Musil completed her Doctor of Management in Organizational Leadership from the University of Phoenix, and holds an M.A. in Organizational Management, a Masters in Information Technology, and a B.A. in Liberal Studies. Liz spends most of her time in Southern California.

Please visit:

lizmusilconsultants.com
drlizmusil.com

www.ingramcontent.com/pod-product-compliance
Lightning Source LLC
Chambersburg PA
CBHW052052190326
41519CB00002BA/200